O9-ABH-375

Renga

Renga

A CHAIN OF POEMS BY

Octavio Paz
Jacques Roubaud
Edoardo Sanguineti
Charles Tomlinson

WITH A FOREWORD BY CLAUDE ROY

TRANSLATED BY CHARLES TOMLINSON

GEORGE BRAZILLER
New York

TO ANDRÉ BRETON

Published simultaneously in Canada by
Doubleday Canada, Limited.

For information, address the publisher:
George Braziller, Inc.
One Park Avenue, New York, N.Y. 10016

Standard Book Number: 8076–0640–5, cloth
8076–0639–1, paper

Library of Congress Catalog Number: 76–184875

First Printing
Printed in the United States of America

CONTENTS

FOREWORD

In April 1969 four poets of Europe disappeared underground for a week. In myth, subterranean retreats augur always the unfolding of a harvest: the harvest of wheat which Persephone descends into Hades to gain as her reward, the harvest of life which Alcestis descends to Tartarus to obtain for her egoistic husband, the harvest of wisdom which all the heroes of initiations go to bring to ripeness and gather in the dark of the underworld.

To tell the truth, the underworld where the Mexican, Octavio Paz, the Italian, Edoardo Sanguineti, the Englishman, Charles Tomlinson, and the Frenchman, Jacques Roubaud, were hidden, was only the basement of a small hotel on the left bank in Paris. No gloom, but plenty of lamps burning calmly beneath their shades. No black poplars, or white cypresses, no fields of asphodel on the banks of Tartarus: just sofas and leather arm chairs. The ghosts of Erebus only served tea here in white jackets. And the muffled rumbling which one made out at times was neither that of the waters of the river of Memory nor the ululating plaint of the Erinnys: it was merely the trains of the métro between the Bac and Solferino stations.

However, once the fixed time of their "cloistering" had run out, the four western hermits climbed back into daylight with the promised harvest: the first European *renga* had been born in Paris.

The renga is a collective poetic form which was extremely popular in Japan where it developed between the Heian period (794–1192) and the Moromachi, in the fourteenth and fifteenth centuries. The rules which then governed the joint elaboration of linked poems or *kusari-renga* had attained great strictness. It was not a question of a pure game of chance, or of the whimsies of a fanciful dialogue. Each poet participating in the communal writing of the renga restricted himself to linking his contribution to that of the poet who handed over to him and thus lent him his voice. If his predecessor or accomplice had just spoken of spring in a haiku, in referring to the month of January, the poet who carried on the chain had to take up the allusion to January and lead it to its conclusion. The third haiku must introduce an idea, related not only to the month of January, but to the notion of spring. The fourth must, however, avoid all allusion to the seasons, etc. Everything in the poem—its diction, the use of homonyms and anagrams—was subject to definite rules. Jacques Roubaud sets forth below the main points concerning this and the principles of continuity and of breaks (breaks within continuity) which governed the work of the assembled poets.

The oldest example of a "collective poem" offered to us by Japanese literature is to be found in the classic mythology of *Manyoshu*, most of the poems of which were composed between 600 and 750 A.D. Neither in the numbers of participants nor the meticulousness of the rules can this primitive "duet" of the Nara period prepare us for what the later flowering of the renga was to become. Doubtless it began as one of those poetic (and amorous) games of question and reply of which Arabian and European courtly poetry offer us equivalents. Otomo Yakamochi (718–785) had written, along with other ladies, alternate poems replying to each other: with Lady Ki, for example. Or with male poets like Otomo Ikenushi. But now it was a matter of something other than alternate poems: here we have one poem written by two people. The first three lines of this *tanka* for two voices were written by an anonymous nun. One finds in their brevity the symbolic implicitness of the themes of water and fecundity, the erotic significance of which has been fairly constant from Sanskrit literature to the poetry of Éluard. The young Japanese nun (I can only think of her as young) wrote:

Someone planted these rice-fields
while damming back the waters
of the river Saho

And Yakamochi completed the tanka with her two concluding lines which are also a concealed erotic invitation and a subtle declaration of love:

Rice of the first harvest
will you eat it alone?

Yakamochi thought, round about 750, that one shouldn't grow rice to eat it alone. Lautréamont, about 1860, thought that "poetry must be made by all, not by one." In 1969 four poets from the four corners of Europe met in Paris to attempt to make, if not poetry by all, at least poetry by several. Charles Tomlinson arrived from Bristol, Sanguineti from Salerno, Roubaud from Dijon and the higher reaches of mathematics. Octavio Paz, as we know, made several detours to get there: certainly, he departed from Teotihuacan, but was delayed en route in the East. Only a short time ago he was ambassador to India. But he is one of those great spirits who prefer honor to honors; and when in Mexico many young people were killed in cold-blooded anger, Paz resigned, proudly, scornfully, and became once more a roving poet, a wandering scholar exiled from everything except poetry (which is everything).

Is the attempt to bring to life once more a cultivated poetic form conceived by a very ancient culture of the far Orient, or at least to find a western equivalent for it, merely a pasttime for leisured and learned poets? It seems to me there is far more to the undertaking of which we have here the first results—an enterprise which Octavio Paz hopes will not end with this poem for four hands. He wants the attempt to continue; he wants other voices to mingle in it, other poets, other languages. Perhaps yearly newcomers could take up the thread, poetry thus regularly renouncing its solo voices in order, from time to time, to bring together several in harmony, going from monody to polyphony, or at least from soliloquy to conversation.

If friendship were simply a matter of one's seeking and sometimes finding another, it would often be a pleasure and sometimes a gain. (To find, or find oneself, is not necessarily pleasurable or beneficial: one must also know whether what one finds is worth while.) But it seems to me that friendship is also to discover, in the happy vagary of meeting, in the contact and the confronting, in the forbearing or risky concurrence of two solitudes, something that at once goes beyond us and connects us. It is difficult to find the word or *words* for this. Those which come to mind first are in danger of being solemn, that is to say hollow; idealistic, meaning flabby; vague, meaning worthless. And I have no settled beliefs of my own sufficient to suggest that what friendship seeks is rather an immanent common denominator, or even a common and shareable objective reality.

In the unending conversation carried on by Octavio Paz with himself and with the friends he has all over the world ("I invent," he says, "the friend who invents me—my likeness"), I have often had the feeling of discovering *places in common* where we did not walk alone, although their spaces were not predefined. We rediscovered together constants in our preoccupations and preoccupations in our constants which were not our own, nor did they seem like our own special prerogative (or solitary confinement). Among Octavio's widely ranging interests, often I recognized my own—or rather: *our* own. His intense ardor, and his passion were entirely *his,* and rarely equaled in warmth and brightness. But in the talk of a man whose culture extends to at least three languages and to their poetry, to many domains of thought and continents of knowledge and wisdom, who in all the certainty of his erudition keeps the joyful freshness of childhood, who recalls the gravity of André Breton and the gay petulance of one of those whose youth seems to last forever because, like the Jew of the fable, they remain endless wanderers; in the natural cosmopolitanism of a mind naturally rooted in his native Mexico, in the gracious alliance of genius with candor and of mischief with boundless generosity, in all of these things which unite to define Octavio Paz, I found myself glimpsing more and more the background of the poet's work, felt myself all the time closer to a man at once open and secret.

Poetry was the most frequent subject of our talks. But a passionate interest in politics, a fascination with the forms of eastern thought and art, returned again and again as leitmotivs between us. I don't pride myself with being the first to talk of such things, any more than Octavio Paz. From Romain Rolland, listening to Lenin with one ear and to Gandhi with the other, to Claude Lévi-Strauss who defines himself in *Tristes Tropiques* as a mind divided between Marxist method and Buddhist philosophy; from André Breton, who pursued all his life the liberty of revolution and the revolution of liberty at the same time as a profound feeling for sacred mystery, to André Malraux, always veering between the temptation of the East and the temptation of revolution—everywhere the deep desire to "change life," in Rimbaud's phrase, and the desire to know how and why the East has seemed at times to lose itself in its own pure and simple *acceptance,* have equally occupied some of the richest and most fortunately disquieted minds of our epoch.

If I look, particularly in reference to Paz, for the meeting point between his revolutionary spirit (fettered, as for all of us, by the monstrous contemporary avatars of revolutionary endeavor) and his attraction toward the forms (extremely diverse, of course) of oriental thought, I seem to glimpse it in that central passion for liberty of the word and for communication by the word, which burns in the work of Paz as poet and essayist and in his life. The injustice of societies is detestable, refusing men the possibility of "inventing" one another, of crossing, in the dialectic of solitude, the instant of communion. For there are no recognitions save among those who are like-minded, and the barriers of hunger, ignorance, and oppression can engender only those who are *unlike* or enemies. It is in order to rediscover the other that a poet like Paz can be straightforwardly political if it seems to him one of the ways to liberate men; or haughtily rebellious against politics if to resign and to refuse seem to him overridingly necessary.

But it is also this wish to rejoin others, without denying the solitude of each being, or abolishing the basic otherness, which explains in Octavio Paz, a Mexican of Indian and Spanish descent, the attraction toward Buddhism, that a-religious religion. I am often disquieted by that allure of eastern religions to which so many uneasy westerners frivolously abandon themselves. Exoticism can be an indulgence, withdrawal, cowardice. Just so, the willingness to revere India in one to whom the religion of his childhood seemed a lot of nonsense. Those who would blush to kneel before a plaster statue of St. Thérèse de Lisieux are led by the fear of death toward vague and distant (and, at the same time, not really *compromising*) superstitions. Kipling has also pointed out the irony of those who, east of Eden, go looking for nice unburdonsome religions, without original sin, without restraints on the flesh, and with a god—it doesn't matter what sort—preferably yellow, and with no prejudices against free love. Orientalist fashions often provide an outlet for shameful religious sentiments looking for a religion whose own distance—and our ignorance—deck out in all the virtues, while the search proceeds for bright new gods to pep up jaded western sensibilities.

But what seems to interest Octavio Paz most in the Buddhist attitude, and in the philosophies which prefigure and join with or derive from it (Taoism, Shintoism, or Zen), lies perhaps in the deliberate refusal to accord belief or absolute values to the permanence of an unchanging spirit: self, ego, soul, jivatman. I can imagine now the "spirited" fun some mocking spirit would have with a poet whose personality shines out (and with what force!) in his least line, in his shortest hemistitch, and yet who feels sympathy toward doctrines which define the I as an ephemeral accident. But the contradiction is only apparent between the I of a great poet—his greatness evident at a first reading—and the lack of credit which this poet himself accords to the notion of the I. And without launching into the descriptive ontology or the philosophy of Buddhism, remaining simply in the domain of literature, I will only say that poets are like trees: they are all united by their roots in the earth and their branches in the sky. There is a moment and a point when the poetry of all peoples is alike. There is a moment and a point when all genius repeats itself, and seems like one great voice which always says the same thing.

I seem to have strayed far from the western renga which I am presenting here. But not so very far. The links of friendship are sometimes the draft of a linked poem, the rules and the form of which have not yet appeared. Talking with Octavio Paz of poetry and beliefs, of Japan and China, Mexico and India, it was natural that the name of another important poet among my friends should come into our conversation, namely that of Jacques Roubaud who was working then on his poems "borrowed" from the Japanese. As in the renga a poet "passes the ball" to the second who passes it to the third, I handed on to Roubaud the ideas and gifts which Paz had given me. It was natural I should come to wish, as they did, that they should meet finally. It was probable they would find points of agreement. Which they did. And it was in the natural course of things that Octavio Paz should wake one bright morning with the idea of bringing together some western poets in order to write a renga with them and with Roubaud. To see. To see if four voices from the four corners could find a basic harmony. To see if each could remain *I* and *you* while at the same time becoming *us*. To see what element—or common elements—would come about from this "united nations" of four poets. To see, in short, what we should hear from this quadrilingual quartet, this international foursome.

When we went to explain the project to Claude Gallimard, he didn't appear over-surprised, or at all reticent, or even alarmed, no more so than that abbot of a thirteenth-century Japanese monastery in a chronicle of the epoch, who, at the request of one of his monks, invited several poets of the region to a renga party "in order to bring into flower, together, a sprig of blossoms."

Some weeks later, the four officiants entered their cell in the rue Saint–Simon. Here they gave voice to what was to be their common venture. And now we have its fruit—the first western renga. I find in it, as in the mirror of a river, the four faces of my companions. Their common taste for set forms, the rules of game, made possible for each one that *jeu* which signifies at the same time liberty, ease of movement, and the strictness of rules. Our Mexican poet is fire, sun, carnage, love, and ashes. Tomlinson is the British and classical descendent of the great English "aesthetes" (it would be better to say "aestheticians"). An Englishman first discovered by the Americans, he shares with his three present accomplices a great admiration for Pound. But he is without doubt the only one of the four to number Ruskin among his masters. And the only one to write poems that are purely descriptive—apparently. (For he says of Constable: "What he saw/Discovered what he was.") Edoardo Sanguineti sets the library on fire—the fire of Marxist–Leninist analysis fed by the books of Babel. Jacques Roubaud is the offspring of *trobar clus* and mathematics. All four of them undoubtedly have masters whom they share, and others peculiar to themselves. But what was born of their toil side by side, and from the experience of writing poetry for four hands, is something quite distinct from a quatrain of Paz plus a quatrain of Tomlinson plus a quatrain of Roubaud plus a quatrain of Sanguineti. It is a complete poem. By whom? Who is speaking? Who is the author? *"What is your name?" asks King Milinda. The monk replies: "They tell me I am called Nagasena. But although parents give names to their children like Nagasena, Surasena, Virasena or Sihasena, they are only designations, denominations, conceptual terms, current appellations, simple names. There's no real person behind them.*" (Saraha, *Dohakosha,* lines 70–112.)

I shall be asked: why take us back to Buddhism? We know well enough without it that the sum of persons is sometimes more than their total: that is, a whole. And that while one speaks of the strings of a violin, one also says "its soul"—which cannot be reduced to these. It was not an oriental guru, but the good Laurence Sterne who caused the narrator of *Tristram Shandy* to be told: " 'My good friend,' quoth I—'as sure as I am I—and you are you.' 'And who are you?' asked he. 'Don't puzzle me,' said I." Here is a puzzle that our four poets got together to solve—happily, one might say.

Claude Roy

INTRODUCTION

In contrast with the conception of a literary work as the imitation of antique models, the modern age has exalted the values of originality and novelty: the excellence of a text does not depend on its resemblance to those of the past, but on its unique character. Beginning with romanticism, tradition no longer signifies continuity by repetition and by variations within repetition; continuity takes the form of a leap, and tradition becomes a synonym for history: a succession of changes and breaks. The romantic fallacy: the literary work as an odd number, the reflection of the exceptional ego. I believe that, today, this idea has reached its end. Two significant indications, among many others: surrealism, in rediscovering inspiration and making of it the very focal point of writing, put into brackets the notion of author; the poets of the English language, for their part—particularly Eliot and Pound—have shown that translation is a process indistinguishable from poetic creation. Our century is the century of translations. Not only of texts but of customs, religions, dances, erotic and culinary arts, fashions, and, in short, all kinds of usages and practices, from the Finnish sauna to yoga exercises. History itself seems to us an imperfect translation—full of gaps, thanks to the stupidity and interpolations of perverse copyists of a lost text which the philosophers, from Hegel and Marx to Nietzsche and Spengler, endeavor to reconstruct. Doubtless other epochs and other people have also translated and with as much passion and care as ourselves (for example: the translation of Buddhist books by the Chinese, Japanese, and Tibetans), but not one of them was conscious of the fact that, in translating, we change what we translate and above all that we change ourselves. For us translation is transmutation, metaphor: a form of change and severance; a way, therefore, of ensuring the continuity of our past by transforming it in dialogue with other civilizations (an illusory continuity and dialogue: translation: transmutation: solipcism). The idea of universal correspondence is returning. Certainly, we no longer see the macrocosm and the microcosm as the two halves of one sphere, but we conceive of the entire universe as a plurality of systems in movement: these systems reflect one in another and, reflecting, they combine like the rhymes of a poem. Thus they transform themselves into other systems, increasingly transparent and abstract, into systems of systems, veritable geometries of symbols, until they reach the point where they cannot be detected by our instruments of observation and end up by evaporating—once more like rhymes which lead into silence and like the act of writing which finishes in nothingness.

Immersed in the world of translation or, more exactly, in a world which is in itself a translation of other worlds and other systems, it is natural that we should have tried to transplant into the West an oriental form of poetic creation. It is scarcely necessary to explain that we have no intention of taking over a genre, but rather of putting into operation a system for the production of poetic texts. Our translation is analogical: we are not concerned with the renga of Japanese tradition, but its metaphor, one of its possibilities or avatars. But why the renga and not some other form—Chinese, Eskimo, Aztec, Persian? In the present moment of its history the West is meeting with the East at various points—meeting without touching, moved by the logic of its own destiny. One of these points is poetry. Not some idea of poetry, but its practice. And the renga is, before everything, a mode of practice. I perceive two kinds of affinity: the first, the element of combination which governs the renga, coincides with one of the central preoccupations of modern thought, from the concerns of logic to the experiments of artistic creation; the second, the collective character of a game, corresponds with the crisis of the notion of author, and with the aspiration toward a collective poetry.

The element of combination consists in the making of a poem by a group of poets; following a circular order, each poet in succession writes his stanza in turn, and his intervention is repeated several times. It is a movement of rotation which, little by little, delineates the text, from which neither calculation nor chance is excluded. I will go further: it is a movement in which calculation prepares for the appearance of chance. I underline that the renga is not a combination of signs, but a combination of makers of signs: of poets. As for collective poetry, one has no need to state that it is one of the modern obsessions. It is an idea that was born with romanticism and which from the very beginning was a contradiction: belief in the anonymous and impersonal nature of inspiration is not readily compatible with the belief in the poet as a unique being. Romanticism exalted simultaneously the I and the we: if the poet is a collective being who sings, the people are a poet with a hundred thousand eyes and a single tongue. Homer is not a real name, but an appellation: it implies a community. Criticism very quickly destroyed the hypothesis of the anonymous, spontaneous, and popular origin of epic poetry. One of Nietzsche's first essays was dedicated to showing that the *Iliad* and the *Odyssey*, by the mere fact of being poems, postulate the necessary existence of a poet, a Homer. Nietzsche's argument is memorable because it contradicts equally the ideas of the romantics and those of the classicists: Homer is not so much a real historical being, as a formal, aesthetic condition of the artistic work. The Homer of Nietzsche is neither the folk of the romantics nor the formidable blind poet of tradition; rather than an author with his own name, he is a consequence of the perfection and unity of the poems. Nietzsche implies that it is not the poet who creates the work, but the opposite. Thus he inaugurates a new conception of the relations between the poem and the poet. However it was the surrealists who brought to an end the idea of the author by resolving the contradiction of the romantics: the poet is merely the place of meeting, the field of battle and of reconciliation of the impersonal and masked forces that inhabit us. Inspired by one of the maxims from Lautréamont's *Poésies*, they affirm that poetry must be made by all and for all. The games of the surrealists had in common their accentuation of the collective character of artistic creation—in the same way that automatic writing rendered manifest the impersonal nature of inspiration. The affinities and analogies between the games of the surrealists and the renga are numerous and profound. More than coincidences, they are rhymes, correspondences: one of the meeting points of East and West. But the differences are not less notable. I will limit myself to pointing out the most important: surrealist activity destroys the notion of the work in the interest of replacing it by the poetic act; in the renga the authors disappear as individuals in the interest of the common work. On the one hand the poetic experience is exalted, on the other, the poem. In the first case: the preeminence of subjectivity; in the second, of the work. In both, the intrusion of chance is a condition of the game, but the rules which originate the game are distinct and even opposed. With the surrealists chance works in an open space: the passivity of critical consciousness. I note in passing the paradoxical character of this passivity: it is voluntary and deliberate, the result of the critical activity of consciousness. The surrealist poet tries to attain that state of absolute distraction which invites and provokes the discharge of concentrated poetic energy. In the renga, chance works as one of the signs of the game—the nameless sign, the invisible current which accelerates or retards progress, the force which turns the steering wheel and changes the direction of the poem. Chance does not appear in a free space but on the track laid down by the rules: its function consists in distributing the regularity of writing by interruptions which distract the poem from its goals and orient it toward other realities. In the surrealist game distraction implies maximum concentration, the *explosion fixe* of André Breton; in the renga maximum concentration produces the liberating distraction, the gap through which the instantaneous flow of poetry bursts forth. Are we confronted by the same chance, or can we designate with the same name two distinct forces having in common only the power of troubling our mental and vital systems?

The practice of the renga implies the negation of certain cardinal western notions, such as the belief in the soul and in the reality of the I. The historic context in which it was born and developed did not know of the existence of a creator god and denounced the soul and the I as pernicious illusions. In the Japan of tradition the social cell, the basic unity, was not the individual, but the group. Further, each in its own way, Buddhism, Confucianism, and Shintoism, fought against the idolatry of the I. For the first it was a chimerical entity: from the point of view of true reality (emptiness) the ego is not so much an infirmity as an optical illusion. Confucianism and Shintoism, for their part, restrict the individual within the double yoke of "filial piety" and loyalty to the feudal lord. For all these reasons, it seems to me that the renga must have offered to the Japanese the possibility of going out from themselves, of passing from the anonymity of the isolated individual into the circle of exchange and recognition. Also it was a way of liberating themselves from the weight of hierarchy. Although it was governed by rules as strict as those of etiquette, its object was not to put a brake on personal spontaneity, but to open up a free space so that the genius of each one could manifest itself without doing harm either to others or oneself.

A practice which contradicts the beliefs of the West, the renga for us was a test, a purgatory in miniature. As there was no question of either a tournament or a competition, our natural animosity found itself without employment: neither a goal to be attained nor a prize to be carried off, no rival to be vanquished. A game without adversaries. From the first day, in the basement room of the Hôtel St. Simon and during the following days, from March the thirtieth to April the third, irritation and humiliation of the I:

—A feeling of abandonment, rapidly changing into disquiet, then into aggressiveness. The enemy is nobody, the anger involves nobody, I am the mask of nobody. One goes from humility to anger, from anger to humility: to write as well as one can, not in order to be better than the others, but in order to contribute to the elaboration of a text the aim of which is to represent neither me nor the others; to advance unarmed across the paper, to lose oneself in the act of writing, to be nobody and oneself at the same time.

—A sensation of oppression: for a Japanese the circle of the renga is a space which opens up, for me it is a snare drawn tight. A trap. I hear the subway trains passing close by. (Clamor: Homeric metaphors for a stormy sea, those of the Vedic hymns on thunder, the iron cataracts of Joyce.) I hear the steps of people entering and leaving the hotel. Renga: school, station platform, waiting-room. Someone comes downstairs and asks us if we have seen a case. Seeing us, each one bent over his sheet of paper, he draws back, murmurs an apology and disappears. Renga: a chain of poems, chain of poems-poets, chain of chains. Murmurs, whispers, bursts of stifled laughter. Drought, electricity in silk, in metal, in the paper on which I am writing. Suddenly, like a curtain which is drawn back, time opens: there appear Marie-Jo, Brenda, Luciana. The wives put an end to this sea storm on dry land. Now we speak aloud, laugh, come up to the surface.

—A feeling of shame: I write in front of the others, the others in front of me. Something like undressing in a cafe, or defecating, crying before strangers. The Japanese invented the renga for the same reasons and in the same manner in which they bathed naked in public. For us, the bathroom and the room in which we write are totally private places, where we come in alone and where we realize acts that are alternately infamous and glorious. In the bathroom we wash, make our confessions, beautify ourselves, purify ourselves, talk to ourselves, spy on ourselves, absolve ourselves . . . each one of these acts, and the rites and excitements which accompany them, has its symbolic (sacramental/excremental) counterpart in the study of the writer: table, lamp, papers, books, chair, typewriter. The difference is that the bath-tub is unproductive whereas in writing we produce texts. Refuse or desires—what is the initial material of the writer?

—A feeling of voyeurism: I see myself manipulating sentences, I see them come together, fall apart, come back into shape. *Les mots font l'amour* on my page, on my bed. Beautiful and terrifying promiscuity of language. Embrace becomes struggle, struggle dance, dance a wave of the sea, the wave a wood. Dispersion of signs. Concentration of insects, black, green, blue. Ants on the paper. Volcanoes, scattered archipelagoes. Ink: stars and flies. Writing-explosion, writing-fan, writing-morass. Pause: he who is writing stops, lifts his head and looks at me: an empty look, a full look, a stupefied look, a lofty look. Writing, playing, copulating: dying? The eyes cease seeing—and see. What do they see? They see what is being written and in seeing it erase it. Writing is reading and erasing written signs in a space which is within and outside us, a space which is ourselves and in which we cease to be ourselves in order to be what or who?

—A feeling of returning: I go down into the magic cave, the cavern of Polyphemus, the hiding place of Ali Baba, the conspirators' catacomb, the cell of the accused, the basement for those punished at school, the grotto beneath the sea, underground room (Proserpine, Calypso), vagina of language, belly of the whale, pit of the crater. The underground workers, gnomes of the word, miners of signs, drillers and dynamiters of meanings. Moles, rats, worms. Venerable serpents, august dragons: guardians of the buried treasure, the iron coffer full of dry leaves, the treasure of foolish wisdom. Shame, pride, mockery. Passage from anguish to laughter. From striking oneself a blow of contrition to a somersault, from isolation to fraternity. Complicity in the common task; respect without respect for others:

I laugh at myself in laughing at you and thus I honor myself and honor you. Community in laughter and silence, community in coincidence and dissidence. Joy underground.

Renga, bath of consciousness, confrontation with myself and not with others: I have undergone neither a struggle nor a victory.

Renga, a spiral, round and round, for five days in the basement of a hotel, each return nearer the light, each circle wider.

Renga, mining-out of language; we make our exit through a gap of silence, on the fifth day, into freezing noon. Dispersion of the spirit, at the crossroads of the boulevard St. Germain and the rue du Bac: Gloucester, Dijon, Salerno, Pittsburgh.

Our attempt naturally enters into the tradition of modern western poetry. One could even say that it is a consequence of its dominant tendencies: the conception of writing as a combined act, the narrowing of the frontier between translation and original work, the aspiration toward a collective (and not collectivist) poetry. And now let me try to bring out the central characteristics of our renga, the trait which distinguishes it radically and totally from the Japanese model: it is a poem written in four languages. I add and I underline: in four languages and in a single language: that of contemporary poetry. Curtius demonstrated the unity of European literature. Today this unity is more visible and more intimate than in the middle ages or in the past century. It is at the same time broader: it extends from Moscow to San Francisco, from Santiago to Sidney. In German, Polish, Roumanian, or Portuguese, the poets of our time write the same poem; and each version of this poem is one that is distinct and unique. Góngora, Donne, the romantics, the symbolists, and our masters and predecessors of the first half of the twentieth century did the same thing. There is not (there has never been) a French poetry, an Italian, Spanish, or English: there was a poetry of the Renaissance, a Baroque poetry, a Romantic poetry. There is a contemporary poetry written in all the languages of the West. If a Frenchman, an Italian, an Englishman, and a Mexican participated in this first attempt to transplant the renga, in future gatherings (for I am sure that other rengas will be written) there will be Russian poets, Germans, Brazilians, Catalans, Greeks, Hungarians . . . all the idioms of the West. On the other hand, although it is desirable, the confrontation with poets of other civilizations seems to me a little more difficult, at least for the present. The reason being that our renga involves two contradictory but complementary elements: the diversity of languages and the community of the language of poetry.

The classic Japanese poem, the tanka, is composed of two verses, the first of three lines and the second of two. Nothing is easier than to divide up a tanka: 3/2, word/echo, question/reply. Once divided, the tanka goes on multiplying. It proliferates by parthenogenesis: 3/2/3/2/3/2/3/2 . . . a verbal fissuring, fragments which separate and link up: the shape described by the renga has something of the slenderness of a snake and the fluidity of the Japanese flute. Looking for a western equivalent of the renga, one thinks of the sonnet: on the one hand it is the sole traditional form which has remained alive up to our own times; on the other, it is composed, like the tanka of semi-independent and separable entities. However, the structure of the sonnet is much more complete than that of the tanka. While the latter is composed of only two verses, the number of divisions of the sonnet varies by virtue of the principle of duplication: the first part of a sonnet is composed of two quatrains and the second of two tercets. In the tanka the relation between the verses is that of odd/even; in the sonnet it is simultaneously even/even and even/odd, since the second section is divided into two "odd" parts. Repetitions, reflections, redundancies, and echoes which permit a great variety of combinations. Rimbaud's "Sonnet des Voyelles" is a single phrase; the Petrarchan sonnet (eight and six lines) is dualistic and extends the themes of courtly love; that of four verses is a cube of sound, a self-sufficient argument, almost a syllogism; that of three terms is dialectical, of the passions: it affirms, denies, and ends in the incandescence of paradox; the Elizabethan sonnet is more music than a verbal monument and, if one compares it with that of Góngora, more inductive than deductive. (The relations between the forms of the sonnet and those of logic are extraordinary and uneasy.) In the Japanese renga linear succession triumphs: the poem flows; in the western renga succession proceeds in a zigzag, by opposition then reconciliation of terms: the poem returns on itself and its mode of unfolding is by way of dialectical negation. In Japan it fluctuates from 3 to 2, from 2 to 3, from 3 to 2; in the West there occurs a continual metamorphosis through the struggle and reconciliation of contraries.

The renga is divided into various sequences or modes. The model for this arrangement is the movement of the seasons or that of the twenty-four hours of the day, the passage from dawn to night. A linear and circular composition, a design of extreme simplicity and extreme elegance which, in the sphere of music, corresponds to melody. We have radically modified these musical and linear characteristics. It is significant that we did this without exactly realizing what we were doing, guided perhaps by the same instinct which led us to choose the sonnet and to conceive of our renga, not as a river which glides on, but as a place of meeting and opposition of different voices: a confluence. We decided to divide our poem into four sequences and that each one of us should set the mood (it would be too much to speak of the theme) of a sequence.* As we had at our disposal only five days in which to compose the poem, we chose to write the four sequences at the same time. I must explain: the first day we wrote the first sonnet of each of the four sequences and so on each day. At the end of our writing, reading the text for the first time, we discovered that we had replaced the linear, melodic order by counterpoint and polyphony: four verbal currents which flowed simultaneously and which wove between them a network of allusions. Each sequence is composed of seven sonnets which must be read one after the other,

* The last sonnet of the last sequence (IV, 7) was not written.

although this order leans on a text composed out of relations of the sequences among themselves. The solo of each sequence (read vertically) moves forward over the ground of a dialogue of four voices (read horizontally). I would like our renga to appear not as a tapestry, but as body in a perpetual state of change, made of four elements, four voices, four cardinal directions which meet at a center and disperse. A pyramid, a pyramidal pyre.

Some readers will object to the renga as a feudal and courtly survival, a fashionable game, a relic of the past. I do not know whether this accusation is right for Japan; in the West the practice of renga could be salutary. An antidote against the notions of author and intellectual property, a criticism of the I and of the writer and his masks. Writing, with us, is a sickness, at once shameful and sacred. Thus to write in public, in the presence of others, seems an intolerable experience. Notwithstanding this, to write in public *with* others carries a quite different meaning: the construction of another space for the manifestation of the plural word, the place of confluence of different voices, currents, traditions. Antidote and contradiction, the renga in the West is neither a method of writing nor a new path for poetry. Renga: a poem which effaces itself as it is written, a path which is wiped out and has no desire to lead anywhere. Nothing awaits us at its end: there is no end, anymore than there is a beginning: all is movement.

Octavio Paz

THE TRADITION OF THE RENGA

The Minase Sangin

still under snow
the mountains are mist-bound
a spring evening

far in the distance running water
near a hamlet of plum-trees

air of the river
against the close willows
spring is appearing

sound of a dragged boat
clear in the clear bright morning

and the moon is it
above the mist-filled fields
in its place in the sky?

hoar-frost in the grass
autumn is coming to its end

insensible deaf
to the cry of so many insects
the grass grows dry

I visited my friend
so bare the ground at his door

lost villages
will the storm come up
into the mountains?

beneath unfamiliar roofs
between solitude and sorrow . . .

This rough paraphrase of the first ten "links" of the famous *Minase Sangin,* the "Renga of the Three Poets at Minase," is offered merely to give an idea (however inadequate) of what constitutes the great originality of this poetic form: the sense of a changing unity.

Multiplication

When Sogi Shokahu and Socho met, during the first moon of the year 1488 at Minase, on the site of the ancient palace of the Emperor Gotoba, in order to compose this poem, the first great epoch of the renga was reaching its end (the second is that of Basho, at the end of the seventeenth century). But during the course of almost two centuries while this initial explosion lasted, there was composed a truly enormous quantity of rengas: rengas of monks, rengas of emperors, ex-emperors, and nobles, rengas of rich lords, rengas of masters of the renga, especially those like Sogi and his pupils, and like the master of this same Sogi, the incomparable Shinkei.

A few facts will show the importance of this multiplication of forms—the population growth of the renga in this period:

—In 1313 a renga session took place in the monastery of Horin at Kyoto. Before they separated, the participants composed one thousand links of renga.

—In 1391 a certain Ashikage Yoshimitsu directed a renga of ten thousand links. This stimulated the ex-emperor, Go-Komatsu, who in 1394 put together, on his own, a renga of the same size. Perhaps one must seek the cause of this solipsistic attitude with regard to the renga in the decrepitude of imperial power during the Muromachi era.

—Finally, from 1433 to 1441, on the instigation of the Shogun in person, Ashikage Yoshinori, a mammoth session of renga took place each year: the poets designated met successively in twenty different places and composed in each five *hyakuin* (a renga of one hundred links).

That is to say that the renga was not then the rare and esoteric exercise of a few hermits inspired by zen. The *raison d'être* of this form lies in the multiplication. At the same time, because of its rapid proliferation, this kind of poetic organism acquired, in the course of its development, rules of an extreme complexity.

Binding Rules

The ground rules of the renga ("connected or linked poems" or otherwise "a chain of poems") are simple: unequal sections (links) of three lines (5–7–5 syllables) and two lines (7–7) are prepared (or improvised) successively by two or several poets, the poem thus composed presenting the following basic feature: any given link of the renga must form a poem along with that which precedes it and this poem must be different from that which it forms with the link which follows it.

The forging together of the links, of the sections, into a whole which is the renga—a poem of poems—was subjected to rules intended to ensure that the dual simultaneous movement of continuity and break was consistent with the aesthetic of the form.

Very quickly, with the increase of the renga, binding rules became so numerous and so difficult to master that there also occurred, from the beginning of the fourteenth century on, a multiplication of collections of rules where, together with examples, directions are also given on how to compose a renga. But it is made clear that one cannot succeed in this without long practice under the guidance of experienced masters.

Collections of Rules

The *shikimoku* (collections of rules) contain formal prescriptions (on use of vocabulary and grammatical forms) and prescriptions as to content: certain things, or certain important concepts must not be used at any cost, or not too often; a list is given of things which may be used once (and once only): young shoots (*wakana*), coltsfoot, peonies . . . others are to figure in two verses (dawn, spring breeze), in three, four, or even five verses (such as general concepts: world, plum blossom, bridge).

Continuity and Breaks in Continuity

The most important rules are those of *sarikiren,* continuity and breaks:

—The seasonal theme, if spring or autumn is in question, must be dominant for three (or five) verses, but only for three if summer or winter are the theme.

—One must give special attention to *uchikoshi wo kiraubeki mono* (things to be guarded against in the verse just gone). For example: pine, bamboo, marsh must be separated by seven links at least. The rules of *sarikiren* are numerous and, for all rengas, a master must see to it that they are constantly abided by.

The Life of Shinkei

The art of the renga reached its first peak, its first achieved aesthetic expression, in the work of Shinkei. As Benl writes: "It is with Shinkei, who wrote virtually only rengas, that Japanese poetry achieved its greatest degree of inwardness . . . The poetic of Basho, two centuries later, is completely in the spirit of that of Shinkei." The life of Shinkei is almost completely lost to view. Araki says: "Shinkei's way of life is entirely unknown to us; veiled, it merges into vagueness, into that tonality of evening light which is in keeping with the renga. Only here and there, like the moon appearing through a break in the clouds, does a fragment of his existence become visible."

Shinkei was born in 1406 in the hamlet of Tai-i, in the Nagusa district of the province of Kii (today the prefecture of Wakayama). In 1463 he returned to his native village and composed a renga of one hundred links in order to achieve spiritual enlightenment. The same year, he concluded his great treatise, *Sasamegoto;* in this he sets forth his poetic ideas; he died, probably in the fourth month of the seventh year of the Bummei era, that is to say in 1475.

The Renga according to Shinkei

It is to Shinkei that I owe the following hints about the deeper sense of the renga form, where for the first time there came together the classic idea of *mono no aware* (the feeling of things) which dominates all early Japanese literature, the chivalric spirit expressed by the romantic speech of the Kamakura era, and the variant aesthetic of contemplative zen, those three currents of Japanese poetry which inspire also *noh.*

The problem of writing renga is this: to ensure the perfect joining together of verse to verse, the construction of the chain, across the movement which carries the poem along through its five phases, labeled by Shinkei *hen, jo, dai, kyoku, ryu* (start, prelude, theme, center, fall).

This is why the main thing for Shinkei is, "to conform to the preceding verse": between the preceding verse and the verse under composition, the extreme tension of the poem must be visible. In other words, a poet writing renga must strain to bridge the gap which exists between the preceding verse written by someone else and one's own.

This is the meaning of *Tanaka*—"for Shinkei, the irruption in the previous verse is more significant than poetic composition itself."

Let us leave the conclusion to Shinkei, with three fragments from *Sasamegoto:*

—"The art of renga is not the art of composing poems, or verses of a poem, but a spiritual exercise to penetrate the talent and vision of another."

—"All the arts are composed only of that which one translates from the heart of things into one's own heart."

—"To follow one's own bent is not the way to experience the indecipherable meaning of others."

Jacques Roubaud

THE UNISON: A RETROSPECT

To undertake the composition of a renga, without the benefit of several centuries of Buddhist self-abnegation behind one, seemed, at first, a questionable venture. How could four Europeans—Octavio Paz is both Mexican and European—suppress their differences of personality for a common literary end? Would the atmosphere be tense with unresolvable divergencies, and calm be shattered by the inevitable collisions of four egos?

But one had overlooked the fact that Octavio Paz had spent many years in India; that Edoardo Sanguineti came from a nation whose family feeling is one of its many strengths; that Jacques Roubaud is a mathematician; that one belonged, oneself, to a country where, at school, children are taught, in their writings (or were up to a generation ago), "Never say *I!*"

One's fears were groundless. Once we had accepted Mr. Roubaud's system of permutations and followed Señor Paz's majestic lead, the poem was the thing. There was dialogue, even debate and a little reciprocal satire, but these things had to submit themselves to the course of the poem as it unfolded, to the pull of other elements within it, and were affected not so much by the need to "be ourselves" as to contribute to a mutual structure. Not that one was any the less oneself: one's self was discovered by the juxtapositions and the confrontations that met it. It was part of a relationship. It was almost an *object.*

Two important considerations affected our efforts: the setting and—if it is possible to divide the two—its literary presences. The immediate setting was the basement of the Hôtel St. Simon, which at once evoked a train of associations with Persephone and the underworld. Emerging from this, one entered the city in one of its most magnificent stretches; a stone's throw from the Louvre and the Tuileries in one direction and from the perspective of the Boulevard St. Germain in another. The architectural presence counterpointed the underground germination. April sunlight over the cleaned stone; obsidian and petrified wood on display in a shop-window; Maillol's statuary disposed in the Tuileries; the heads of Hermes above the Quai D'Orsay Station (bluish in the evening light, their vague helmets like cascading hair); the bust of Le Nôtre, "auteur de ce jardin," beside the Jeu de Paume; Henri Rousseau's mathematical trees just coming into leaf—all these stood in the vicinity of, seeming to ask admission into, our communal revery. And the literary presences gained access without knocking—Baudelaire in the first four lines, Rimbaud, Lautréamont, and, witnesses of our common heritage, Arnaut Daniel, Dante, Donne, Quevedo. Donne's unmoving lovers of *The Extasie* became the Etruscan couple of the Ville Giulia: they embodied the erotic side of our poem, celebrated the personal and at the same time translated it into the sculptural. For our theme was both dream and stone, the unpremeditated and the architectural, water and watercourse: we had come together to unite four disparate voices in a single form —the sonnet. Our activity seemed paralleled by the city: a host of fragmented activities flowing past and challenged by the forms of Mansart, Lemercier, Le Vau, Bruant. The city also became Persephone, rousing from its darkness into a season of possibilities. It became woman, the other, the outside, but the outside in the process of being metamorphosed (while resisting metamorphosis) by the conditions of our waking dream.

We rose from our underworld, not on the third, but on the fifth day, returning each to his separate milieu, to compose the final sonnet of the sequence which he had begun. (Edoardo

Sanguineti deemed *his* sequence complete: his silence was his sonnet.) This sonnet was to be "all one's own work," but divided as one now was from those other voices, one was still governed by the circumstances in which the work had taken shape. One still found oneself speaking with a communal voice: speaking with a communal voice one found—once more—one's self.

Charles Tomlinson

Renga

Renga can be read in either of two ways, the first horizontal and the second vertical:

I 1	II 1	III 1	IV 1
I 2	II 2	III 2	IV 2
I 3	II 3	III 3	IV 3
I 4	II 4	III 4	IV 4
I 5	II 5	III 5	IV 5
I 6	II 6	III 6	IV 6
I 7	II 7	III 7	

I_1

El sol marcha sobre huesos ateridos:
en la cámara subterránea: gestaciones:
las bocas del metro son ya hormigueros.
Cesa el sueño: comienzan los lenguajes:

and the gestureless speech of things unfreezes
as the shadow, gathering under the vertical
raised lip of the columns' fluting, spreads
its inkstain into the wrinkles of weathered stone:

Car la pierre peut-être est une vigne
la pierre où des fourmis jettent leur acide,
une parole préparée dans cette grotte

Principi, tomba e teca, sollevavo salive de spettri:
la mia mandibola mordeva le sue sillabe di sabbia:
ero reliquia e clessidra per i vetri dell' occidente:

I_1

The sun advances over bones benumbed:
in the underground room: gestations:
ants ooze already at the mouths of the métro.
An end of dreams, and the gift of tongues begins:

And the gestureless speech of things unfreezes
as the shadow, gathering under the vertical
raised lip of the columns' fluting, spreads
its inkstain into the wrinkles of weathered stone:

For the stone is perhaps a vine
the stone where ants jet out their acid,
a spoken word that readies itself within this cave:

Princes! tomb and showcase, I heaved up ghostly saliva:
my jaw gnawed its syllables of sand:
I was relic and clepsydra through the panes of the West:

I_2

Ma i miei profili ridevano dentro poltrone vuote, sopra pareti sepolte.
la mia mano bruciava nel cerchio bianco della fotografia di Marie-Jò:
il 30 marzo ero già un teschio, nell' ombra del suo immenso cappello
di feltro:

Ce matin-là je sortis au bras d'un cheval harnaché
laissant mes empreintes dans la cendre d'une cigarette
comme le cœur d'une plante verte au fond d'un guide touristique

Scherzo dopo andante (e perché no?) scherzo ambulante
venditore di reliquie, *of rotten apples, Persephone, perspex,*
Ceres and breakfast cereal, columns of ink
and (published by Feltrinelli) Il cappello di feltro *by Sanguineti:*

Mientras escribo caen sobre mi lunas en pedazos,
uñas arrancadas a leopardos disecados, cráneos, risitas,
dispersión de un osario verbal, lluvia de anécdotas.
En mi página corren en corro graciosos ratones.

I_2

But my profiles were laughing in empty armchairs, above buried
walls,
my hand burned in the white circle of the photograph of Marie-
Jo:
March thirtieth I was a skull already, in the shadow of her
immense felt hat:

That morning I went out on the arm of a horse in harness,
leaving my imprints in the ash of a cigarette
like the heart of a green plant in a travel guide:

Scherzo dopo andante (*e perchè no?*) *scherzo ambulante,*
venditore di reliquie, of rotten apples, Persephone, perspex,
Ceres and breakfast cereal, columns of ink
and (published by Feltrinelli) *Il Cappello di Feltro* by San-
guineti:

While I write, scraps of moons shower over me,
nails torn from stuffed leopards, skulls, little laughs,
dispersion from a verbal boneyard, rain of anecdotes,
across my page run graceful mice in their ring-of-roses.

I_3

And you will bury neither the sun in its progress nor the vine:
Out of perspex debris, post-card landscapes,
Spools of forgotten films—hand
In hand Eros and laughing Ceres reassume the land:

Commentario (in greco) le 120 journées
—come, al Port St. Germain, con Octavio,
con Jean, il 31 marzo— Jean disse: ma ci sono tre livelli (nelle Philosophie
dans le boudoir): *e il secondo livello (scenico) non è praticabile; ecc. —*
figure strettamente allacciate:
praticano il secondo livello:

[*Nota (¿en nahuátl?): Occidente dice:* «Eros and Ceres,
hand in hand etc» but *practica (sin decirlo) los* 120 journées...
Sade: lo que no decimos; Rousseau: lo que no hacemos.]

[*Commentaire (1180): Arnaut:* «pois floris la seca verga... *(etc...)*»
et plus loin «son Dezirat c'ale Pretz en cambra intra...» *(et Dante*
« comme se noie une pierre dans l'herbe... ») (kokoro no kami —
l'obscurité du cœur!)]

I_3

And you will bury neither the sun in its progress nor the vine:
out of perspex debris, post-card landscapes,
spools of forgotten films—hand
in hand Eros and laughing Ceres reassume the land:

Commentary (in Greek), the *120 Journées*—as, in the Port St. Germaine, with Octavio,
with Jean, March thirty-first—Jean said: but there are three levels (in *Philosophie*
dans le boudoir): and the second (theatrical) level is not practicable; etc.
figures tightly embracing:
they are practicing the second level:

[Note (in Nahuatl?): the West says "Eros and Ceres
hand in hand etc.," but practices (without saying so) the *120 Journées.*
Sade: what we don't say; Rousseau: what we don't do.]

[Commentary (1180?): Arnaut: "since the dry rod flowered" (etc.)
and further on: "his *Désirée* whose price brings her into the bedroom . . ." (and Dante:
"as a stone is drowned in grass . . .") (*kokoro no kami*—the heart's obscurity!)]

I_4

Ni les objets, ni les anecdotes, mais les sons, leurs traces
leurs manières de mémoire : des phrases qui se divisent
(non la *langue, mais* cette *langue) ceci est le seul arbre*

(A través the pane of abstraction and contemplation
we gazed at the moon of changelessness but then,
girded the weapons of the autumn frost over our garments of forbearance...)

Ma Jacques ha portato i libri giapponesi, il terzo giorno; e io ho preso il primo libro (Tr. by D.K.), *la prima volta, e l'ho aperto, e ho letto (p. 138):*
"The room is supposedly so dark that...";
e la seconda volta (p. 426):
"In the darkness enveloping the room and his heart";
e ancora, la terza volta (p. 42):
"smoking to the right";
e io ho acceso una Benson, in the dark room (Special Filter):

Ash and the third day's darkness. Not "speech", but this
speech of contingencies and quiddities—held
and heard (can the measure hold its own?)
stilled in the concourse of asymmetries, raw sorrel sundown.

I_4

Neither objects nor anecdotes, but sounds, their trace
their modes of remembrance: sentences dividing
(not speech, but this speech) this is the sole tree:

(Through "*the pane of abstraction and contemplation*
we gazed at the moon of changelessness, but then,
girded the weapons of the autumn frost over our garments of
forbearance . . .")

But Jacques brought Japanese books the third day; and I took
the first book (tr. by
D.K.), the first time, and opened it and read (p. 138):
"*The room is supposedly so dark that . . .*";
and the second time (p. 426):
"*In the darkness enveloping the room and his heart*";
and again, the third time (p. 42):
"Smoking to the right";
and I lit a Benson, in the dark room; (special filter):

Ash and the third day's darkness. Not "speech," but this
speech of contingencies and quiddities—held
and heard (can the measure hold its own?),
stilled in the concourse of asymmetries, raw sorrel sundown.

I_5

«y al cabo de los siglos me descubro
con tos y mala vista» [*Baudelaire à l'hôtel d'York, aujourd'hui Etna Hotel* (lava sobre los gatitos de A.)] «barajando
viejas fotos» *presque effacées (comme d'une râpe humide)*

(Rumor de río en cadenas: el metro.
Yo pienso en ríos de lodo nácar
que sobre inmensas páginas de polvo —Punjab, Bihar,
Bengala— escriben su discurso insensato...)

Mythless I enter my present, my native land
and coming night, desireless now, save to give
back all that I have taken with a disruptive hand

Tra rovine che sono immondizie: scatole di latta, ritratti
di attori, sonetti, sterco:
la sera di una domenica, nella campagna
tranquilla, nell'ora del tramonto, quando si risale in macchina:

I_5

"And at the end of epochs, I find myself once more
with a cough and bad eyesight" (Baudelaire at the Hôtel d'York,
today
Hôtel Etna (A's kittens beneath lava) "sorting through
old photographs" almost effaced (as with a damp file):

(Rumble of a river in chains: the métro.
I think of rivers of nacreous mud,
over immense pages of dust—Punjab, Bihar,
Bengal—scribbling their senseless discourse . . .)

Mythless I enter my present, my native land
and coming night, desireless now, save to give
back all that I have taken with a disruptive hand:

Among ruins which are filth: tin cans, portraits
of actors, sonnets, excrement:
a Sunday evening in the quiet
country, at the hour of sunset, when you get back into the car:

I_6

verso il telegiornale della notte, il poker, l'ultimo libro
di Butor, il magnetofono con le voci dei bambini,
qualche distratta carezza, il dentifricio, il pigiama:

O Sade, Rousseau — utopies sexuelles —
Avec un requin, oui. Mais, mon cher Lautréamont
(O mathématiques sévères!) on ne peut s'accoupler
avec un éléphant :

Sobre las utopías en retazos, la ropavejería
erótica, la chatarra de la era industrial,
caen las pavesas del incendio genital:
¡llueve, incandescencia, soneto, jardín de llamas!

Pleus sur le carnage des arbres entre les termes
de la phrase souterraine si loin
d'un soleil qui pèse dans les branches

I_6

Toward night news on the television, poker, the last book
of Butor, the tape-recorder with the childrens' voices on it,
a few absent-minded caresses, toothpaste, pajamas:

O Sade, Rousseau—utopies sexuelles—
Avec un requin, oui. Mais, mon cher Lautréamont
(O mathématiques sévères!) on ne peut s'accoupler avec un éléphant:

Over tattered utopias, over the erotic
second-hand clothes shop, debris of the industrial era,
fall sparks from the genital conflagration:
rain on! —incandescence, sonnet, garden of flames:

Rain into the carnage of the trees, among the words
of the subterranean sentence   so far away
from a sun which lies heavy among the branches:

I_7

Calina respiración de la colina, azoro
en el yerbal (bajo tu arco la noche duerme,
velan tus brasas): peregrinación serpentina:
la boca de la gruta, lápida que abre, abracadabra,
la luna: entro en la alcoba de párpados, tu ojo
disuelve los espejos: hamam *de los muertos*
y resurrección sin nombre propio:
soy un racimo de sílabas anónimas.

No hay nadie ya en la cámara subterránea
(caracola, amonita, casa de los ecos),
nadie sino esta espiral somnílocua,
escritura que tus ojos caminantes,
al proferir, anulan — y te anulan, tú mismo
caracola, amonita, cuarto vacío, lector.

I_7

Hazeshape hillscape breath, a startling
amid undergrowth (below your arch night is asleep,
your ashes keep their vigil): a serpentine wandering:
mouth of the cave, graveslab (abracadabra) that the moon
opens: I enter the eyelids' alcove, your eye
dissolves the mirrors: *hamam* of the dead
and resurrection with no name of my own
I am a cluster of anonymous syllables.

There is no-one now in the underground room
(seashell, ammonite, house of echoes),
no-one save for this somniloquent spiral,
script that your traveling eyes,
in uttering, annul—and you they annul, yourself
seashell, ammonite, empty room, *lecteur*.

II_1

Aime criaient-ils aime gravité
des très hautes branches tout bas pesait la
Terre aime criaient-ils dans le haut

(Cosí, mia sfera, cosí in me, sospesa, sogni: soffiavi, te-
nera, un cielo: e in me cerco i tuoi poli, se la
tua lingua è la mia ruota, Terra del Fuoco, Terra di Roubaud)

Naranja, poma, seno esfera al fin resuelta
en vacuidad de estupa. Tierra disuelta.

Ceres, Persephone, Eve, sphere
earth, bitter our apple, who at the last will hear
that love-cry?

II_1

Love they kept crying love gravity
of the topmost branches far below heavily hung the
earth love they kept crying up there

(This is the way, my sphere, you dream suspended within me:
tender, you breathed into being a sky, and I seek inside myself;
  seek your poles, to see whether
your tongue is my wheel, *Tierra del Fuego, Tierra de Roubaud*)

Orange, apple, breast, sphere, all inherits at last
the emptiness of the *stupa*. Earth powders away.

Ceres, Persephone, Eve, sphere
earth, bitter our apple, who at the last will hear
that love-cry?

II_2

Ashes and end.
A clouded moonrise. Vague, vain
implosion, a seepage, ghoststain:

He vuelto de tu cuerpo al mío (la hora)
tú me miras desde el tuyo (es deshora)

(ho scritto arcobaleni di miele per le tue fragili ginocchia,
quando ero Simon du désert, *dentro funebri cinematografi:*
a mezzanotte, cortesi passanti confermavano le nostre strade)

Hors du noir dans un chemin noir nous entrions
comme les dents de l'encre dans un buvard
(il le fallait : la lune seiche était au bord de l'obscur)

II_2

Ashes and end.
A clouded moonrise. Vague, vain
implosion, a seepage, ghoststain:

I have returned from your body to my own (time)
from yours you look at me (is untimely)

(I have written rainbows of honey for your fragile knees,
when I was Simon Stylites, in funereal cinemas:
at midnight, kindly passers-by helped us find our way)

Out of the gloom a gloomy path we entered
like the teeth of ink into a blotting paper
(and so we must: the squid moon was at the edge of dark)

II_3

Ama gritaban ama la ligereza
ya en reposo ama la fijeza
en pleno vuelo — la gravedad de la presteza

La moitié de l'eau s'assombrissait   la moitié
de l'air   une ronde noire entrait dans l'eau
et la nuit était une moitié de lac

And love, a command no more, to each one
the way lies clear through the comity of vine, of stone:

(attraverso luoghi che sono anni, di fronte a vetrine illuminate
che sono dialoghi spezzati dal montaggio, ritorni, ancora, per rue du Dragon, scendi le tue scale:)

II_3

Love they kept crying love swiftness
already at rest   love the unmoving
in full flight—the gravity of speed:
Half of the water grew dark   half
of the air   a black round entered the water
and night was half a lake:

And love, a command no more, to each one
the way lies clear through the comity of vine, of stone:
(through places that are years, before lit-up show windows
which are dialogues split-off from montage: you return, once
more, by the rue du
Dragon, you come down your stairs:)

II_4

(ti riconosco nel vino, nella pietra:
leggo, con te, oracoli elementari — alla stazione Havre-Caumartin, per
esempio,
sta scritto, in matita nera, in grande:
ON T'OBLIGE PAS [A] TE LE LIRE :)

Together we read (fourmis perdues) *the scraps*
and stones of the city to discover there

La couleur réduite d'une munition de fleurs
livres de lierre traversés d'un blanc rapide
qui flambe sur la quiétude des palissades

Libros de yedra, libros sin horas, libros libres:
cada página un día, cada día el asombro
de ser vino y piedra, aire, agua, palabra, parpadeo.

II_4

(I recognize you in the wine, in the stone:
I read with you elementary oracles—at the Havre–Caumartin
   Station, for example,
someone has written, in black pencil, in capitals:
ON T'OBLIGE PAS [A] TE LE LIRE:)

Together we read (*fourmis perdues*) the scraps
and stones of the city to discover there

The subdued color of a bombardment of flowers
books of ivy crossed by a rapid white
which flares over the quiet of the palisades

Books of ivy, books of no hours, liberty's books:
each page a day, each day the marvel
of being wine and stone, air, water, utterance, flutter of eyelids:

II_5

(mi distendo sopra il tuo corpo, come queste parole
sopra il secondo verso di un sonetto rovesciato:
ti stringo con le deboli dita di queste mie parentesi)

je te serre sans force avec de l'ozone avec de la paille
je répète ta musique au début de chaque laisse
jour à jour (les nuits sont cette canso capfinida)

abres y cierras (paréntesis) los ojos como este texto
da, niega, da (labios, dientes, lengua) sus sentidos:

in this branchwork labyrinth of glance and feature,
these lines that are life-lines,
these veins vines.

II_5

(I stretch myself out over your body, like these words
along the second line of a mirror sonnet:
I grasp you with the weak fingers of these brackets of mine)

I grasp you without force with ozone with straw
I repeat your music at the start of each *laisse*
day by day (the nights are this *canso capfinida*)

you open and close (brackets) your eyes, and this text
gives, denies, gives (lips, teeth, tongue) its meanings

in this branchwork labyrinth of glance and feature
these lines that are life-lines,
these veins vines:

II$_6$

These hands restore us
to a natural and thus more human
because more than human lineage:

Al cruzar el Pasaje de la Visitación, me dijo:
«Mira a la luna.» Y yo la miré — a ella, no a la luna.

Et mon visage était reflet dans l'eau (au creux
d'une main) et elle-même, peut-être, l'eau,
le creux de l'eau où j'avais mal vécu:

(dentro i paesaggi, o lí, appena in margine: i paesaggi della terra
che sono le rivoluzioni:
e anche sotto i paesaggi, dentro le stanze sotterranne,
qui, tra il giuoco e l'utopia, tra le poesie e le verità):

II_6

These hands restore us
to a natural and thus more human
because more than human lineage:

Crossing the *Pasaje de la Visitación,* she said:
"Look at the moon," and I looked—at her, not at the moon:

And my face was a reflection in water (in the hollow
of a hand) and she herself, perhaps, the water
the hollow of water where I had lived badly:

(inside landscapes or there—just—in the margin: landscapes
  of the earth
which are revolutions:
                    and also beneath landscapes, inside under-
  ground rooms,
here, between game and utopia, between poems and truths):

II_7

aime... criaient-ils   aime   c'est le repos
de l'encre   c'est la boue à la caféine
(tête limpide par capillarité)

et retourne vers la fatigue spacieuse
les blancs ou mouches négrières   tes mains
grises gabardines sur ses branches   tes

cloques de paysages   aime   quand tout
est aveugle   tout est impossible   tout

est   « herbe coupée de ses racines   si
une eau t'invite   suis là » aime   criaient-ils
d'arbres confus

II_7

love . . . they kept crying   love   it is the ink's
day of rest   it is mud in caffeine
(head limpid through capillary attraction)

and go back to a spacious tiredness
the blanks or nigger-trading flies   your hands
gray gabardines on the branches   your

blights on the landscape   love   when everything
is blind   everything impossible   everything

is   "grass cut back to the roots   if
water invites you   follow it"   love   they kept crying
          out of confused trees

III_1

The given is ground. You are bound by it
as the eyes are bound—by a frame of nearnesses
surrounding things half-seen: thick, bare
calligraphy and confusion of boughs on air:

est donnée la confusion des arbres
d'infiniment petites poussières
mouches sur le grain du papier herbes
bouches blanc dans le sol de la vue.

Confusa ritorni, confusione diffusa, insetto incerto,
scabbia per ogni mia palpebra, spada per l'iride, scena
nuda: il tuo ombelico è l'occhio del mio albero, aperto
paesaggio di catene, di fruste: siringa per la mia vena:

Suelo, árboles, marañas, ombligo, rayo fijo
(Ares y Eros): la escritura respira : mar nupcial.

III_1

The given is ground. You are bound by it
as the eyes are bound—by a frame of nearnesses
surrounding things half-seen: thick, bare
calligraphy and confusion of boughs on air:

It is given, the confusion of the trees
of infinitessimal particles of dust
flies on the grain of the paper, grasses
mouths   blank in the ground of sight:

Confused, you come back, confusion diffused, uncertain insect,
scabies for each of my eyelids, sword for the iris, bare
scene: your navel is the eye of my tree, wide
landscape of chains, of whips: hypodermic for my vein:
ground, trees, thickets, navel, fixed ray
(Ares and Eros): the writing breathes—nuptial sea.

III_2

Lo dado — de la piedra al mar a ti: vaiven de sílabas
en busca de un hogar. (¿Soneto = amonita?)

perché le tue labbra sono labirinti di marmellata,
gabbie di fosforo per gli obelischi del mio zoo,
trombe di grammofono per il pennello delle mie dita,
nidi per le mie vespe, giardini per i miei topi morti:

je déambule parmi tes lices de patelles
je suis banquise de tes fourrures, je suis doublon de tes boucles
je m'essouffle contre la laine que tu pavanes
gong j'oscille sous les dièses de tes rires

and in the to and fro of syllables in search
of marriage, meaning, what I find
is the given woman, the mythless presence
and quotidian certainty of your heart and mind.

III_2

The given—from the stone to the sea to you: traffic of syllables
in search of a home. (Sonnet = ammonite?)

because your lips are labyrinths of jam,
cages of phosphorus for the obelisks of my zoo,
gramophone horns for the brush of my fingers,
nests for my wasps, gardens for my dead mice:

I saunter among your tourneys of patellas
I am the icefloe of your furs, I am the doubloon of your curls
I am breathless against the wool you flaunt in
gong   I oscillate beneath the sharps of your laughter

and in the to-and-fro of syllables in search
of marriage, meaning, what I find
is the given woman, the mythless presence
and quotidian certainty of your heart and mind:

III_3

Ho segnato sopra la mia fronte le rughe del tuo utero,
i morbidi anelli del tuo muschio mestruale:
ho versato lividi liquori dentro le pagine dei tuoi calendari:
ho coltivato il fungo e la felce sopra le spiagge dei tuoi laghi:

(Alguien, sin nombre, bajó, extraviado, a la cámara
subterránea, diciendo: je cherche une valise. *Y yo vi,*
otra vez, la antigua gruta (cenozoico) entreabrirse y,
entre la maleza oscura, la espuma y sus profecías.)

Le même ensevelissement féroce nous sépare de la pierre
où chantent les fontaines suaves de l'ultraviolet
les bicyclettes et leurs mômes blondes, les rosiers des ambassades
les vitres douchées de bière solaire, pastorale:

fountains and draperies of Goujon, water in flowing stone:
city of Mansart, Lemercier, Le Vau, Bruant.

III$_3$

I have inscribed on my brow the wrinkles of your uterus,
the soft rings of your menstrual moss:
I have poured livid liquors into the pages of your calendars:
I have cultivated mushroom and fern on the beaches of your lakes:

(Somebody nameless, property mislaid, came down to the room
underground, saying: *Je cherche une valise*. And I saw
another time, the ancient cavern (cenozoic) half-open and—
between the obscure undergrowth—the foam and its prophecies.)

The same cruel burial separates us from the stone
where the soft fountains of ultraviolet sing
the bicycles and their would-be Bardots, the rose-trees of the embassies
the panes drenched in a solar pastoral beer:

fountains and draperies of Goujon, water in flowing stone:
city of Mansart, Lemercier, Le Vau, Bruant.

III_4

Pleine de rêves? Pleine de mesure. *Surreal Narcissus*
the river and the buildings are passing you by!

"worn out by dreams"! je me tourne vers d'autres abeilles
(orages didactiques, pieuvres des dénombrements)
l'exercice des preuves est une drogue placide
le crissement de la craie une sibylle sans lèvres

¿Narciso ante su lago o Euclides
trazando figuras en la playa?
Afuera, el río y sus palacios ahogados,
afuera, los trenes, los aviones, les départs — *¿dónde es afuera?*

nuoto dentro il tuo fiume, ancora una volta:
chiudo tutti i miei occhi, per specchiarmi
dentro la faccia incerta dei figli
che non sono nati, le tue ostriche di acqua dolce.

III_4

Pleine de rêves? Pleine de mesure. Surreal Narcissus
the river and the buildings are passing you by!

"*Worn out by dreams*"*!* I turn toward other bees
(didactic storms, octopuses of enumerations)
the exercise of proofs is a placid drug
the grating of chalk   a sibyl without lips:

Narcissus before a lake or Euclid
tracing figures in the sand?
Outside, the river and its drowned palaces,
outside, trains, planes, *les départs*—where is outside?

I swim once more in your river:
I shut all of my eyes, to mirror myself
in the uncertain faces of sons
who are not yet born, your freshwater oysters.

III_5

Where—and what? What is "outside"? That
in whose creation I had no part, which enters me now
both image and other; marriage or loss
of memory: the Place des Vosges under a sun I did not choose:

per subire telefonate e diapositive, les manières de table, *gli amici, i*
classici annotati:
i gesti d'amore in una camera di rue Montalembert
(3e étage), *nelle prime ore di un pomeriggio d'aprile, nel '69:*
e scegliere, poi, alla fine in fretta, in mezzo a tutto questo, come si
sceglie un vestito chez Tiffany:

c'est l'extérieur des choses — bien disposées en extérieurs —
acceptant les compliments de gestes, de larmes, de fureurs factices
pendant que la forme prémonitoire que nous portons depuis le premier
moment
se fige peu à peu dans une dernière exubérance de bouteilles

Afuera es nuestra América cotidiana.
Tambien nuestro adentro está fuera.

III_5

Where—and what? What is "outside"? That
in whose creation I had no part, which enters me now
both image and other; marriage or loss
of memory: the Place des Vosges under a sun I did not choose:

to submit to telephone calls and slides, *les manières de table,*
   friends, the classics
annotated:
                acts of love in a room in rue Montalembert
(*3e étage*) in the early hours of an April afternoon, in '69:
and you choose, then, at last in haste, in the middle of all this,
   as one chooses a dress *chez Tiffany:*

which is the exterior of things—well disposed as exteriors—
accepting the compliments of gestures, tears, factitious furies—
while the premonitory shape which from the first moment we
   wear
hardens little by little into a last paunchy exuberance of bottles:

Outside is our quotidian America.
It is outside, also, our within—we populate or abandon it:

III_6

Lo dado es el afuera (el horizonte en que nos internamos)
y el adentro (la semejanza que inventamos) Lo dado : lejanía.

choses reçues de loin en loin
au-delà de balles et de ponts
la vitesse fouille dans l'herbe
des gares retirées de cigales

ma pronti per partire, ormai:
con le prenotazioni largamente confermate
i franchi sfavorevolemente cambiati, gli indirizzi nel taccuino,
i libri con le dediche:
sotto un'evidente spinta centrifuga verso questa
o quella Università, lontano:
e con una cravatta nuova:

Inventamos? — decipher, rather: text
and irrefutable quotation: gift
of the statuary messengers that crown
(ignored) the gables of the d'Orsay Station.

III_6

The given is the outside (the horizon we enter)
and the inside, too—the resemblance we invent. The given: the
faraway:
things received out of the distances
beyond the flight of balls and bridges
speed ransacks the grass
stations far removed from crickets:

but ready to depart now:
reservations more than once confirmed,
money exchanged (unfavorably): addresses in one's notebook,
books with inscriptions:
back, by a manifest centrifugal thrust, to
this
or that farflung university:
and with a new tie:

Invent?—decipher, rather: text
and irrefutable quotation: gift
of the statuary messengers that crown
(ignored) the gables of the D'Orsay Station:

III_7

Speech behind speech: language
that teaches itself under the touch and sight:
in the night-bound city, language of light
uncovers spaces where no spaces were;
between the image of it and your face:
language of silence; sufficiency of touch,
o my America, my new-found-land explored,
unspeaking plenitude of the flesh made word;

measure and dreams: through the conduit of stone
the flux runs gleaming: rivermap of a hand:
stained-glass world contained by a crystal:
the faces inhabiting a single face,
Persephone, my city: from whose prodigal
ground, branches a tree of tongues, twining of voices,
a madrigal.

III$_7$

Speech behind speech: language
that teaches itself under the touch and sight:
in the night-bound city, language of light
uncovers spaces where no spaces were;
between the image of it and your face:
language of silence; sufficiency of touch,
o my America, my new-found-land explored,
unspeaking plenitude of the flesh made word:

measure and dreams: through the conduit of stone
the flux runs gleaming: rivermap of a hand:
stained-glass world contained by a crystal:
the faces inhabiting a single face,
Persephone, my city: from whose prodigal
ground, branches a tree of tongues, twining of voices, a madrigal.

IV_1

1 rouge *(nella mia nebbia)*; *dolce*; *4* noir(s): *(severe!)*, *inverno*, *tempo*:
mia neve, e inferno, inferma: in ferma, in decente, tu, materia;
ma (un cavallo sellato si allontana): tu sei numero, niente (verso destra):

alfabetos, números: nous dirons vos naissances latentes,
cereales de Ceres, granadas de Proserpina,
semillas, pueblos, razas enterradas: ¡tiempos!

And the darkness feeds the days, and that swaying roof
despoiled now of its pitch of leaves, awaits
the glow at the heart of fog that will engender
more than number, and Ceres swell-out the ciphers:

o sweet ciego rojo limp al punto de la rota
quand, plus-de-bleu plus-de-noir toi séquence de céréales
nombre du puits des feuilles ouvres en tremblant (tremor
at pitch of neve) *ta lueur de louve* (aloof!) *sémillante*

IV$_1$

1 *rouge* (in my mist); sweet; 4 *noir*(*s*): (severe!), winter,
weather:
my snow, and inferno, infirm: in you, firm, seemly matter;
but (a saddled horse goes off into distance): you are number,
nothing (toward the right):

alphabets, numbers: *nous dirons vos naissances latentes*
cereals of Ceres, pomegranates of Persephone,
seed, peoples, races beneath earth: epochs!

And the darkness feeds the days, and that swaying roof
despoiled now of its pitch of leaves, awaits
the glow at the heart of fog that will engender
more than number, and Ceres swell out the ciphers:

sweet blind and limp at the center of the wheel
when, no-more-blue no-more-black you, cereal sequence,
number of the well of leaves, opens (trembling) (tremor
at snow pitch) your sheen of a she-wolf (aloof!) spilling life:

IV$_2$

Si tu griffes t'éloignant, une trace [*ongle de neige*
dessous: un ceps une cigogne (quelque chose qui change)]
dans l'air qui poisse t'en allant [*la fumée poisse les couleurs*
blanches (comme si le cœur tombait dans la goule de la nuit)]

but the hardness of what is real refuses
that syntax of deliquescence. Relation poises, and
the tenderness of what is dual baptises
colours clean: in the eyes' paradise the nail a moonshard:

fijezas cambiantes, durezas que se disipan
apenas nombradas, archipiélagos errantes,
corales de coral en el caracol de tu oído.

4 rouge(s) *(nella mia notte); arida; 1* noir: *(matematiche!); oh, mia musica!*
ancora nasconde il mio Nilo la sua dura testa di mostro:
(io vedo zoccoli); (io ascolto code): giuoco a scacchi; (2 blanc[s]):

IV_2

As you go off into the distance, if you scratch a trace (nail of
snow
under it a vine, a stork [something which changes])
in the air which makes sticky as you go away (the smoke makes
sticky the colors
blank [as if the heart fell into the maw of night]):

but the hardness of what is real refuses
that syntax of deliquescence. Relation poises, and
the tenderness of what is dual baptizes
colors clean: in the eyes' paradise the nail a moonshard:

changing solidities, hardnesses which vanish
as soon as named, wandering archipelagoes,
coral chorales in the conch of your ear:

4 *rouge*(*s*) (in my night); arid; 1 *noir* (mathematics!); oh,
my music!
once more my Nile conceals its hard head of a monster:
(I see hooves); (I hear tails); I play chess; (2 *blanc*[*s*]):

IV_3

1 (une unique) syllabe sur cette feuille ni
noire ni rouge 1 (syllabe) cheminant
(a capo chino) *1 syllabe (pourquoi?) douloureuse questionnant :*

out of this subterranean Babel, babble
and beginning place, place that for the first
time is weighed and heard incarnate, as word on word

appear your names *(luminosi);* your woman's ciphers: *i tuoi segni;*
(i tuoi colori); le luci delle tue voci: ah, come precipito, in te, mia gola!
Come mi trascino (3 vert*), sopra le terrazze del tuo regno!*
mio dizionario, mia algebra, mia lingua sola!

Sílabas emigrantes, burbujas
semánticas, álgebra pasional:
pirámide de catorce escalones (Eras)
y Palabra una — convergentes transparencias.

IV_3

1 (one single) syllable on this leaf neither
black nor red 1 (syllable) going its way
(*a capo chino*) 1 syllable (why?) sad, questioning:

out of this subterranean Babel, babble
and beginning place, place that for the first
time is weighed and heard incarnate, as word on word

appear your names (luminous); your woman's ciphers; your
 signs;
(your colors); the lights of your voices: ah, how I fall headlong
 into you, my throat!
how I drag myself (3 *vert*) across the terraces of your kingdom!
my dictionary, my algebra, my sole tongue!

Wandering syllables, semantic
bubbles, algebra of the feelings:
pyramid of fourteen tiers (eras) and single
word, transparencies converging on each other:

IV_4

Yo por un túnel de vocales húmedas,
tú por un jardín de reflejos, un enrejado de miradas.
En una claridad nos encontramos. El sol
come mi sombra en el circo leonado de tu vientre.

E io dicevo:
così, felici, noi, a correre, in questo vento, via! e sopra questi cavalli; tra questi colori del giorno; in queste musiche! :
(Tomlinson, che dormiva nel bagno, disse: è la natura); (e Jean disse, tutto severo: ma ci vuole politica, qui);
[*e io dicevo: ma è già possibile (la verità)*]:

But Baucis and Philemon (superannuated lovers) disappeared
In the collectivisation of gardens and vines, and the inspector of gramophones
(1 rouge aveugle) *rolled up the landscape for the manufacture of window-blinds.*

IV_4

I beside a tunnel of humid vowels
you by a garden of reflections, an espalier of glances.
We met in a clearness of light. The sun
eats my shadow in the lion-colored arena of your belly:

and I said:
happy, like this, we hurrying, in this wind, and off!
riding
these horses; among these the day's colors; in these
bursts of music!:
(Tomlinson, sleeping in the bathroom, said: in
nature's bosom); (and Jean said,
all serious: they need politics here);
(and I said: but it's possible now [truth]):

but Baucis and Philemon (superannuated lovers) disappeared
in the collectivisation of gardens and vines, and the inspector of
gramophones
(1 *rouge aveugle*) rolled up the landscape for the manufacture
of window-blinds:

(pourtant)
Et je disais
oui heureux à courir
ici dans ce vent
dans (aussi)
pas de vent pas de couleur pas de
température (une limace)
musique une et je disais
abstraite

(however)
And I said
yes happy to run
here in this wind
in (also)
no wind no color no
temperature (a slug)
music an and I said
abstract

IV$_5$

Decía (A noir, E blanc, I rouge, V vert...): "O equals
X-ray of her eyes; it equals sex." *Omega azul (digo):*
cero rebosante, gota de tiempo diáfano, presencia sin reverso.

He said she said (green-swaying roof above
'this dialogue of one'): 'We saw by this it was not sex:
City, we saw not what did move' :

così siamo rimasti, anni e anni, muti, senza espressione, caricati
sopra il nostro sarcofago:
i bambini, figure ancora intatte,
piangono nel bassorilievo
i nostri nomi sono indecifrabili,
le tue labbra sono screpolate:
ma, in noi, i turisti vedono amore:

couple de la Villa Giulia *(oiseaux étrusques : bleus puis rouges)*
de l'un vers l'autre, sourire — cependant des fontaines criaient,
bassine bouillante de mûres sur des braises (Capodimonte,
seins de la Vénus au chapeau de Lucas Granach, serpent pagaille)

IV_5

He said (*A noir, E blanc, I rouge, U vert . . .*): *"O equals X-ray of her eyes: it equals sex."* Omega blue (I say): brimming zero, iota of diaphanous time, Presence without reverse.

He }
She } said (green swaying roof above
"this dialogue of one"): "We saw by this it was not sex:
city, we saw not what did move":

We stayed like this, year on year, silent, expressionless, stretched above our sarcophagus:

infants, faces still intact,
weep on the relief;
our names are indecipherable,
your lips are chapped:
but the tourists make out love in us:

Pair of the Villa Giulia (Etruscan birds: blue then red)
exchanging their smile—meanwhile the fountains cried out,
the basin bubbling over with blackberries onto the embers (*Capodimonte,*
breasts of Lucas Cranach's Venus with a hat, disorder's serpent)

IV$_6$

cette phrase en méandres qui s'achemine vers sa fin perplexe
d'images citationnelles, ronces (soliloques polémiques)
cette ligne de banderilles, cet œsophage de latex
guide nécromant qui s'écrit arborescente   Impression d'Afrique

e come mi sono modificato:
[*e, per concludere, un Charles Pope*
(*un* Tory anarchist), in the collectivisation of poetry
(*con un ilozoiste conscient, ecc.: e tutti alla stessa tavola*):
oggi, Pop-poet, *in questa cripta, per questo* jeu de mots]:

I have become four voices that encircle
a common object, defining a self
lost in a spiral of selves, a naming:

y la espiral se despliega y se niega y al desdecirse se dice
sol que se repliega centro eje vibración que estalla astro-cráneo
del Este al Œste al Norte al Sur arriba abajo fluyen los lenguajes

IV_6

This meandering phrase making its way to its irresolute close
with its images in quotes, briars (polemical soliloquies)
this line of banderillas, this windpipe of latex
necromantic guide which tree-like writes itself out, Impression
of Africa

and what changes I've undergone:
(and, to conclude, a Charles
Pope
(a Tory anarchist), in the collectivisation of poetry
(with *un ilozoiste conscient,* etc.: and all at the same table):
today, Pop-poet, in this crypt, for this *jeu de mots*):

I have become four voices that encircle
a common object, defining a self
lost in a spiral of selves, a naming:

and the spiral unfolds, denies and, in countersaying, says itself
sun which draws back on itself, center, axis, vibration which
explodes, star-skull:
from east to west to north to south above below flow forth the
languages

DATE DUE